MOUSE COLORING BOOK

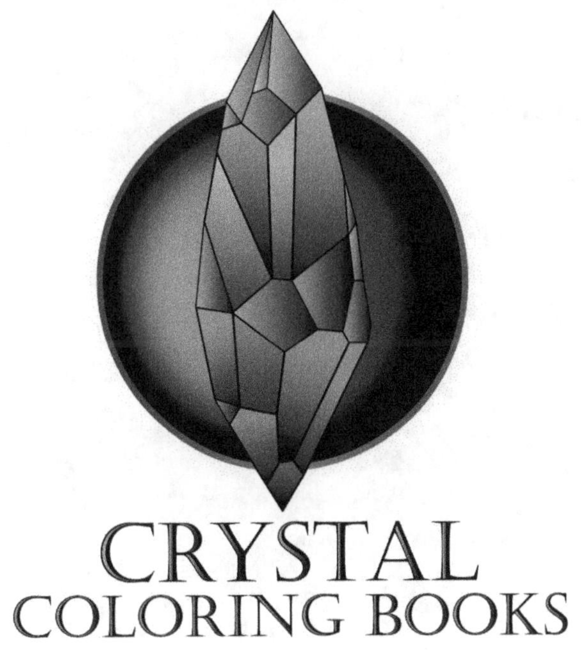

CRYSTAL
COLORING BOOKS

ISBN-13: 978-1977631831
ISBN-10: 1977631835

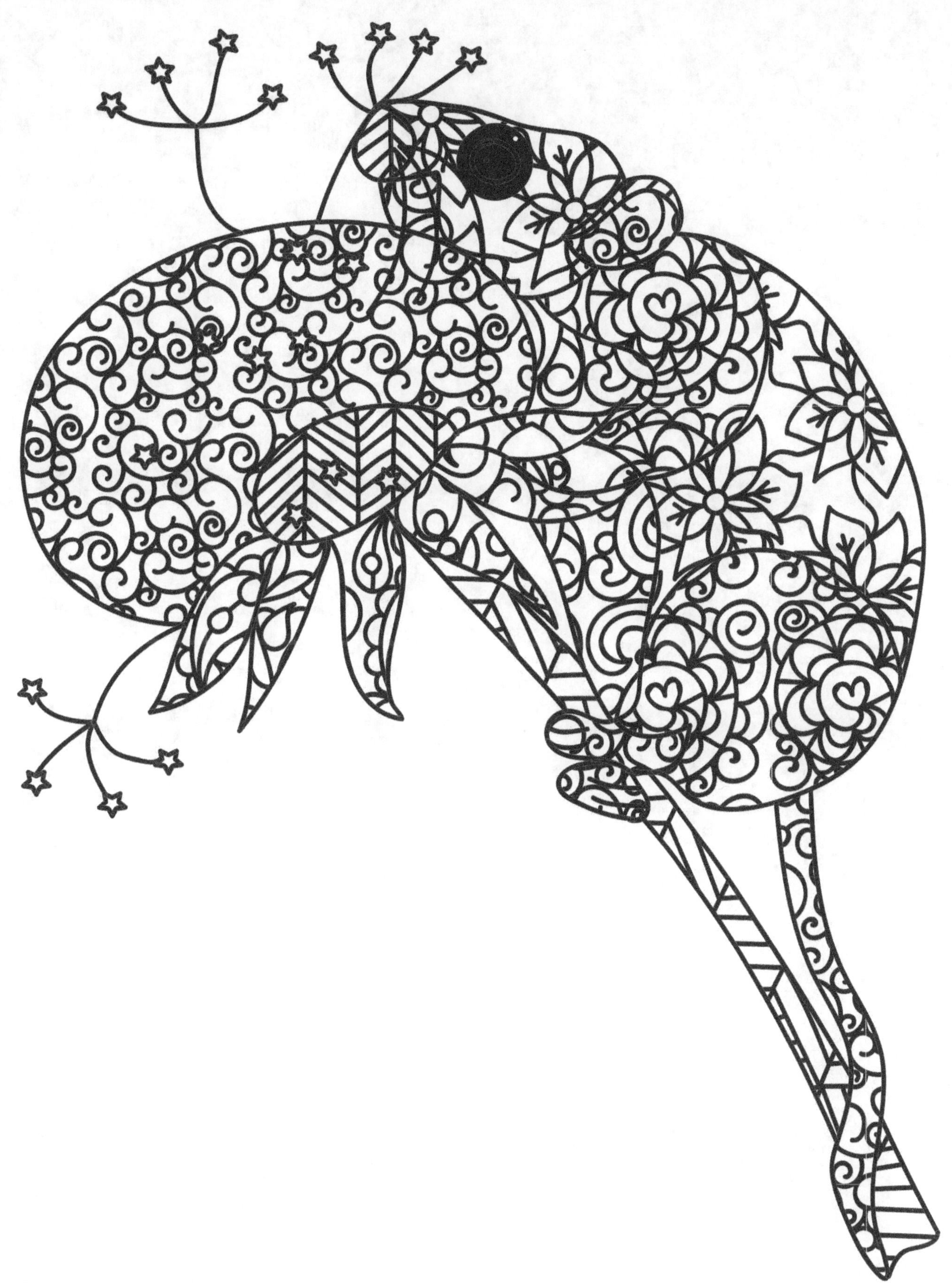

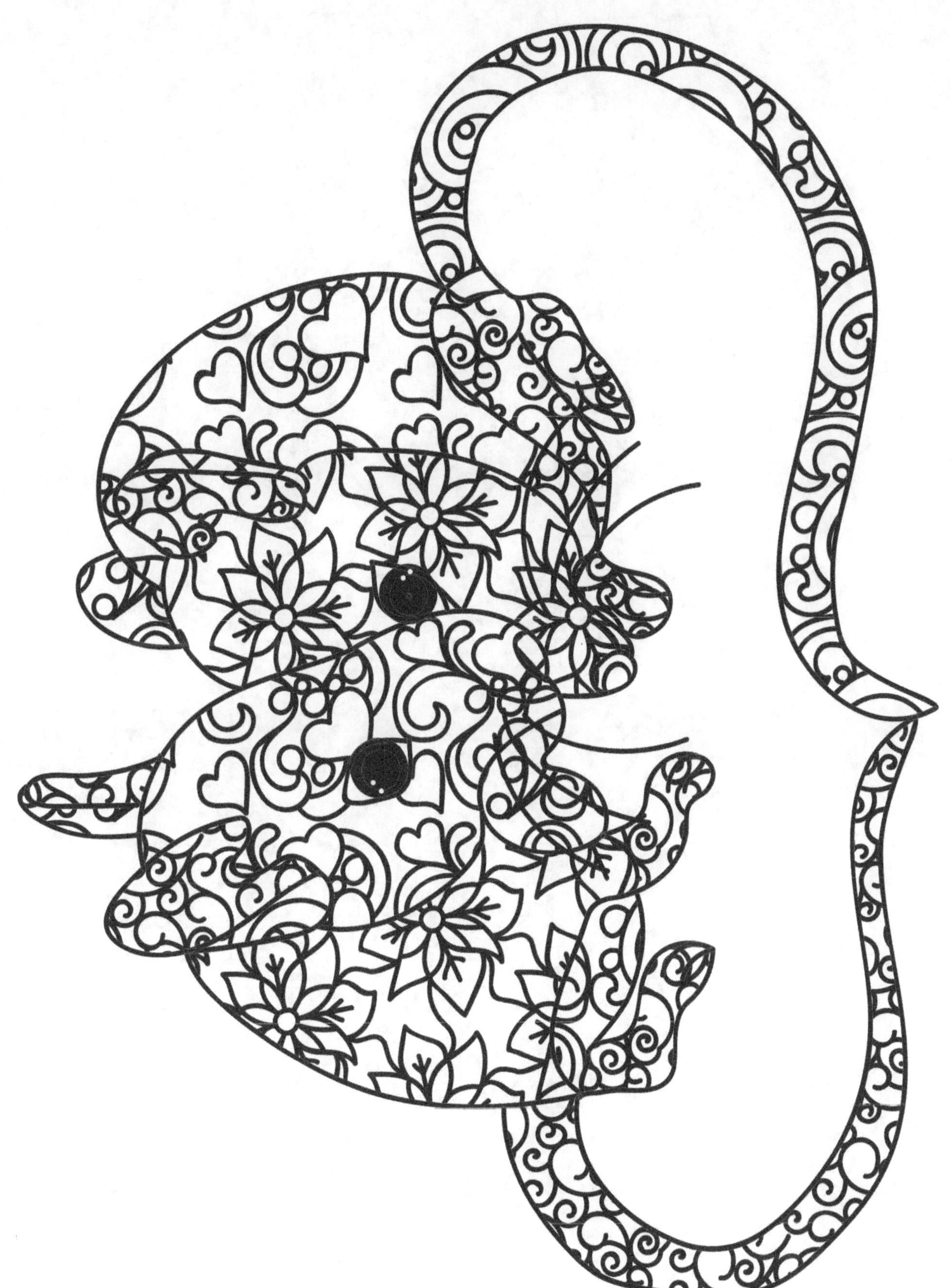

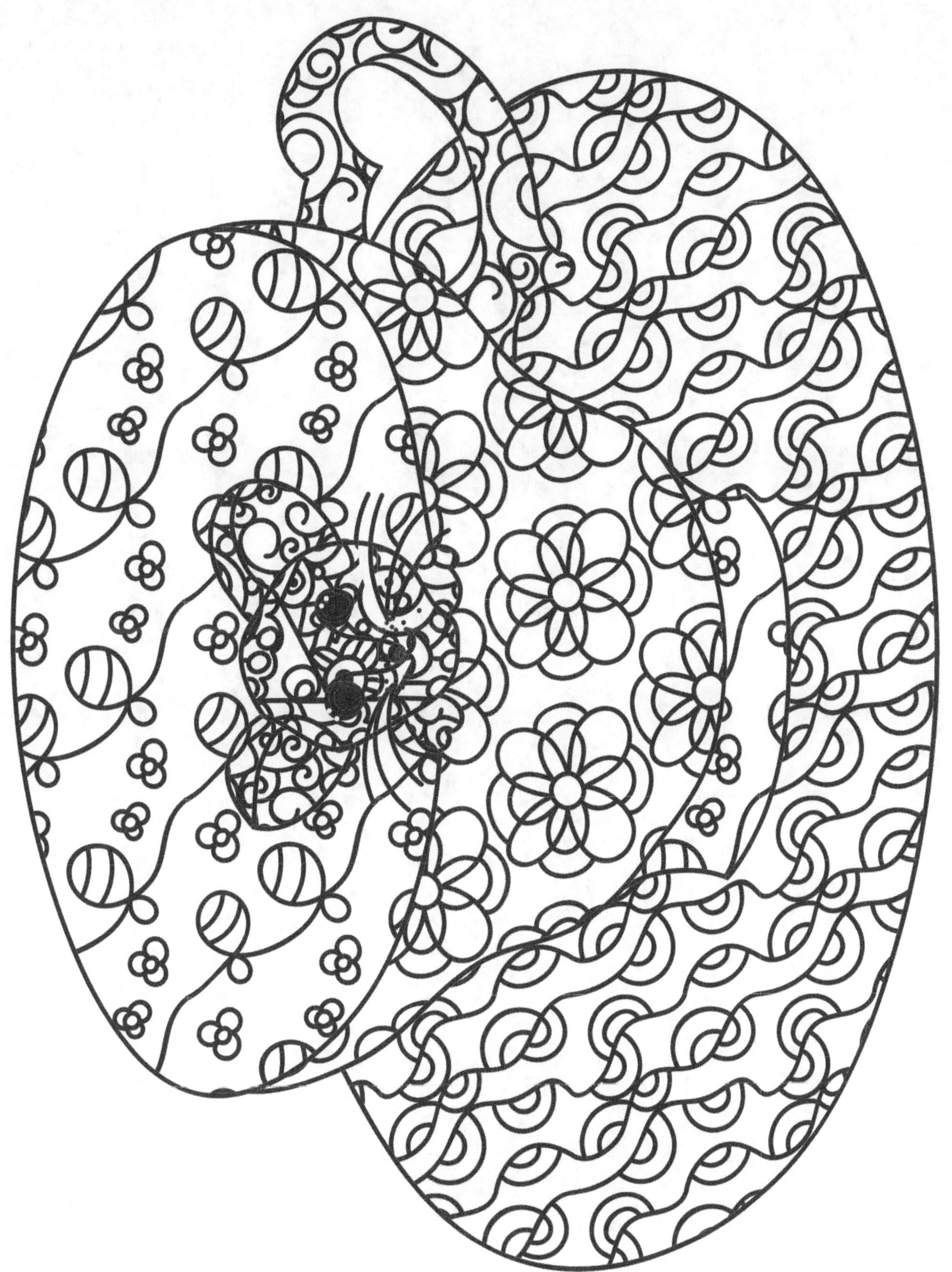

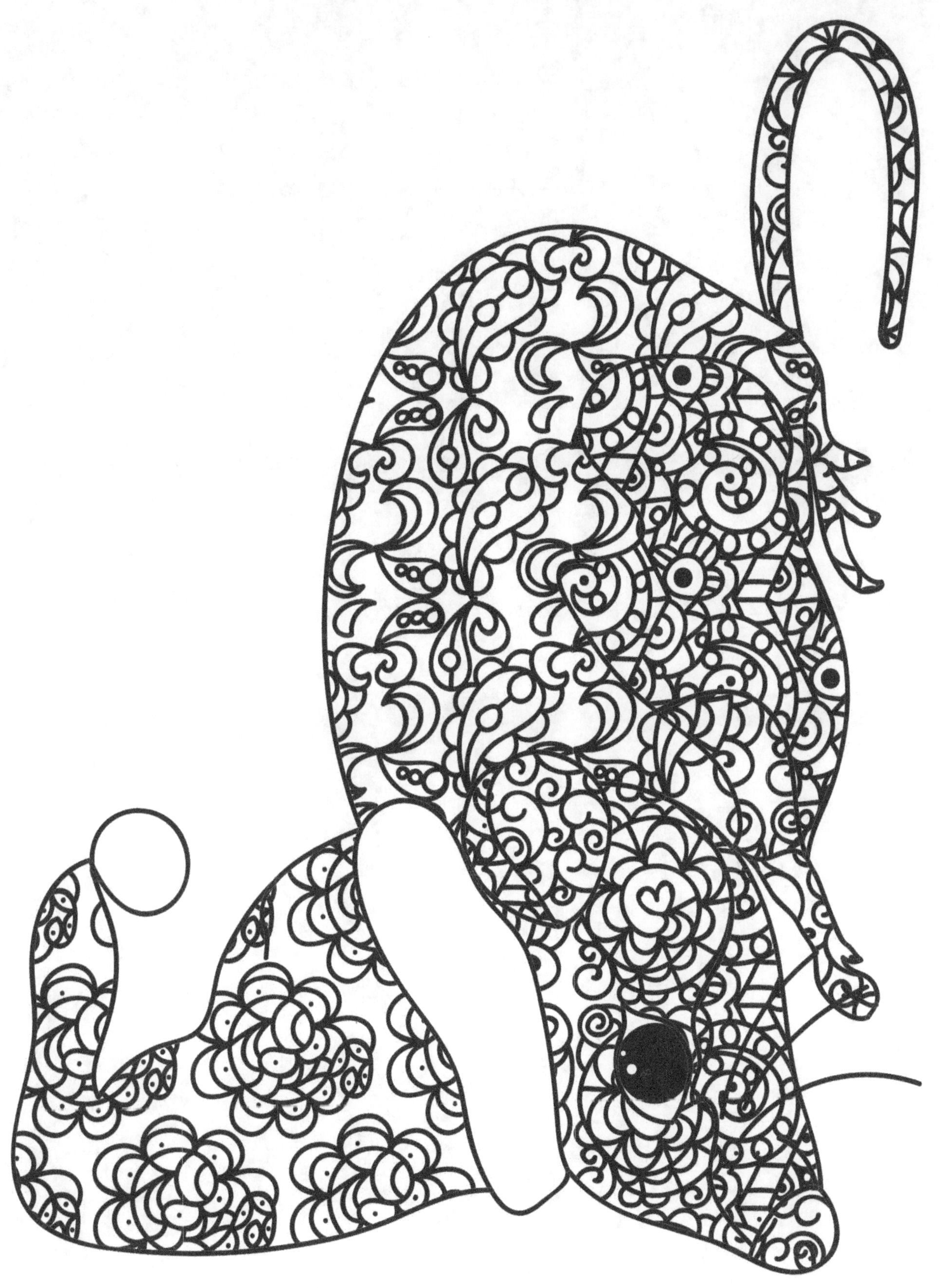

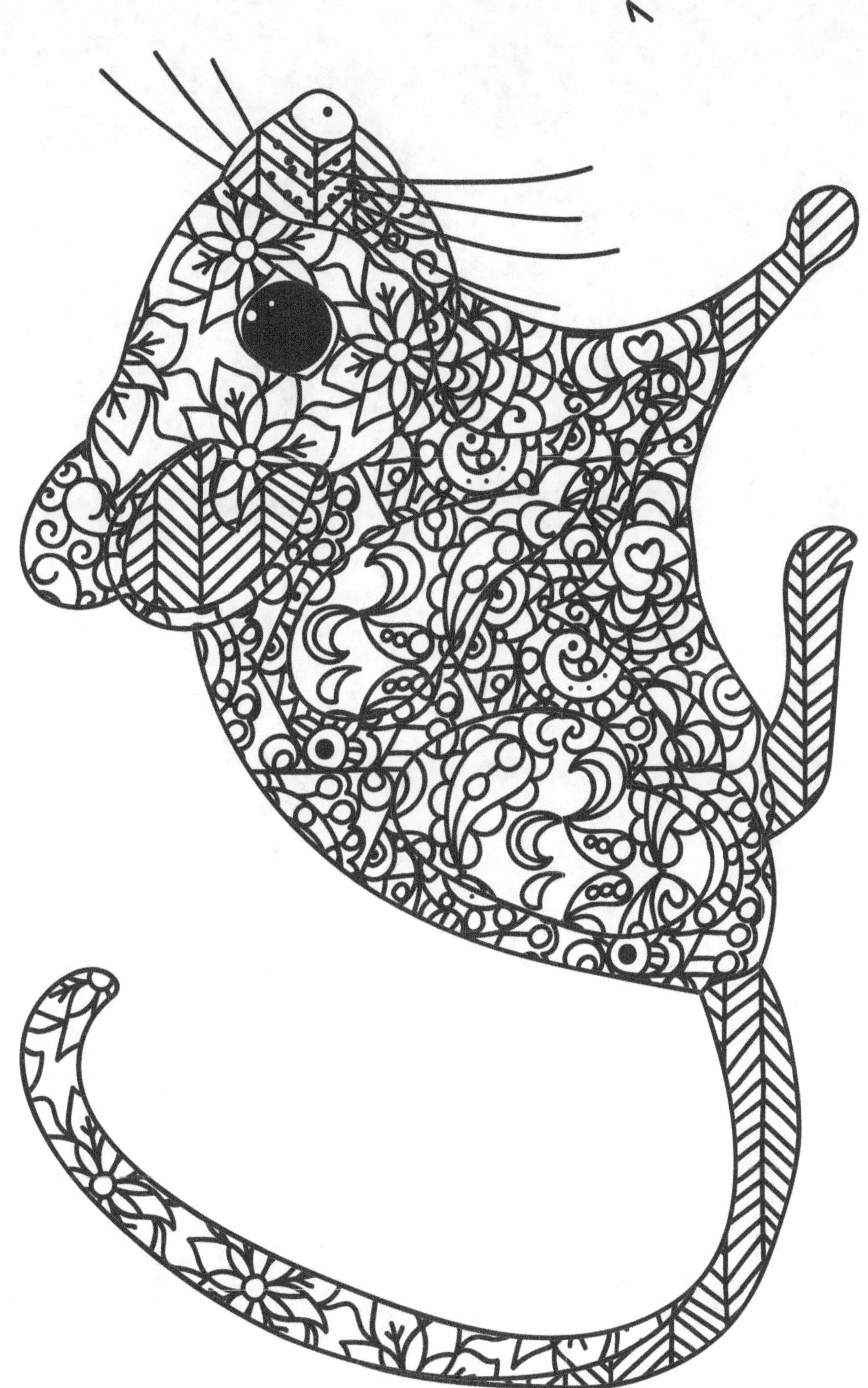

COLOR TEST PAGE

COLOR TEST PAGE